WHAT IS MANGA?

Manga is a broad Japanese term, literally meaning "entertaining visual," though it is most often used to refer to comics and graphic novels created in Japan. However, the manga art form is no longer restricted to Asian stories or settings—it's become a global phenomenon!

In recent years, manga's popularity has exploded in the U.S., lining the shelves of bookstores, filling home libraries, and stuffing backpacks across the nation. In fact, TOKYOPOP introduced of the first extensive manga publishing program in North America, evolving manga entertainment and changing the way people experience pop culture. One of the most common misconceptions about manga is that it's all the same. TOKYOPOP is proud to publish a very diverse selection of titles that appeal to people of vastly different ages and interests.

In this special TOKYOPOP Sneak, you'll find previews from three of our newest series: Kat & Mouse, Mail Order Ninja, and Sea Princess Azuri. We believe that TOKYOPOP's creators are expanding manga's artistic boundaries and creating a new vision for manga entertainment, and we hope you agree.

Learn more about these and other TOKYOPOP series at www.tokyopop.com.

Enjoy the Manga Revolution!

Table of Contents

Free Comic Book Day Sneaks

Layout and Lettering - Lucas Rivera
Cover Layout - Christian Lownds

Editor - Rob Tokar
Digital Imaging Manager - Chris Buford
Managing Editor - Lindsey Johnston
Editorial Director - Jeremy Ross
VP of Production - Ron Klamert
Editor-in-Chief - Rob Tokar
Publisher - Mike Kiley
President and C.O.O. - John Parker
C.E.O. and Chief Creative Officer - Stuart Levy

A  Manga

TOKYOPOP Inc.
5900 Wilshire Blvd. Suite 2000
Los Angeles, CA 90036

E-mail: info@TOKYOPOP.com
Come visit us online at www.TOKYOPOP.com

ISBN: 1-59816-806-1

First TOKYOPOP printing: May 2006
10 9 8 7 6 5 4 3 2 1
Printed in the USA

Story by:
Alex de Campi
Art by:
Frederica Manfredi

Sometimes the smart girls finish first!

When Kat's dad gets a job as a science teacher at a posh private school, things seem perfect—that is, until her rich, popular classmates shove her to the bottom of the social heap just for being smart. And bad turns to worse when an anonymous student blackmails Kat's dad to give the class better grades! Can Kat and her new friend, a rebellious computer nerd named Mouse, find the real culprits before Kat's dad loses his job?

IN STORES NOW!

Genre Icon: Mystery
Rating: A (All Ages)
Price: $5.99

MOUSE HUANG'S GUIDE TO

THE NERD-NERDS:

Brains: 5
Evil: 1
Cool: 1
Sports: 1

"Will own us all in 10 years!"

Special Move: Future-fu!
Info: Band, chess club, MMO games.

THE CHLOETTES

Brains: 2
Evil: 5
Cool: 5
Sports: 4

"Kills with one look!"

Special Move: Fashion Snub of Death!
Info: Chloe is the most popular girl in the class, and her dad's a Senator. She and Mimi and Ruth are a total clique.

The Peace-Heads

Brains: 3
Evil: 2
Cool: 4
Sports: 3

"Shield of impenetrable smoke!"

Special Move: Incense Cloud!
Info: Listen to Phish. Go barefoot a lot. Vacation in Guatemala to build schools and buy ethnic sweaters.

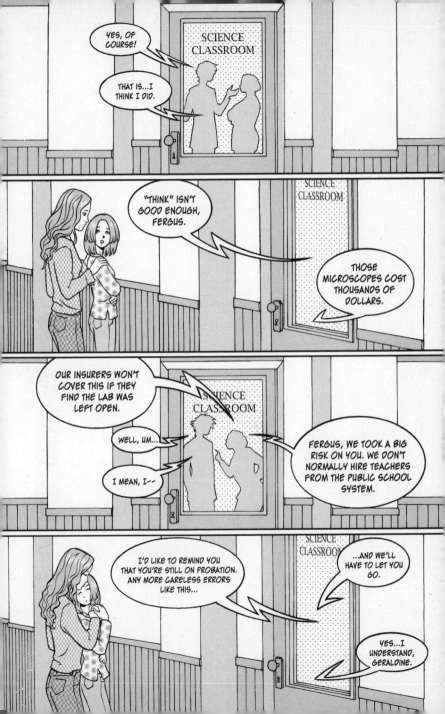

CRKT

IT'S OKAY, CLAIRE. IT'S OKAY.

MAIL ORDER

CHERRY CREEK, INDIANA 47472
JUN 13 2006 USPS

USA $5.99 (×8)

NINJA™

Story By
Joshua Elder

Art By
Erich Owen

NO. 1

What could be better than an imaginary friend? Your very own NINJA!

Story by:
Josh Elder
Art by:
Erich Owen

From the winners of TOKYOPOP's Rising Stars of Manga #5 . . .

Meet Timmy McAllister, a normal kid who lives in the 100% pure vanilla town of Cherry Creek, Indiana (pop. 23,745), where everyone and everything is frighteningly normal... until the day Timmy orders his very own ninja! Who needs imaginary friends—or even man's best friend—when you can have your very own Ninja? Timmy, and the town of Cherry Creek may never be the same!

In stores this JUNE!!!

Genre Icon: Comedy
Rating: Y (Youth)
Price: $5.99

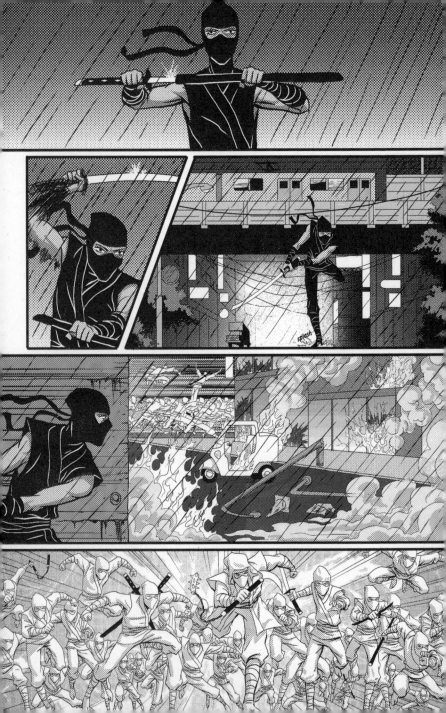

BIO

NAME: Felicity's Entourage
OCCUPATION: Hangers-on
FAVORITE PERSON: Who do you think?

PRESS

CHOP

CUT

ZWISSH

KRAK

THUD

BIO

NAME: Yoshida Jiro
OCCUPATION: Legendary ninja warrior
FUN FACT: Jiro once had a promising music career and was dubbed the "Japanese Barry Manilow" by critics.

DRAMACON™

Sometimes even two's a crowd.

When Christie settles in the Artist Alley of her first-ever anime convention, she only sees it as an opportunity to promote the comic she has started with her boyfriend. But conventions are never what you expect, and soon a whirlwind of events sweeps Christie off her feet and changes her life. Who is the mysterious cosplayer that won't even take off his sunglasses indoors? What do you do when you fall in love with a guy who is going to be miles away from you in just a couple of days?

CREATED BY SVETLANA CHMAKOVA, CREATOR OF MANGA-STYLE ONLINE COMICS "CHASING RAINBOWS" AND "NIGHT SILVER"!

Preview the manga at:
www.TOKYOPOP.com/dramacon

Should she save the world...or follow her heart?!

sea princess
azuri

Story & Art by
Erica Reis

Azuri is the
mermaid
princess and
the only royal
heir of the
Orcans, a
race of whale-
merpeople
that lives in a fantastic
world deep within the ocean. Azuri is
betrothed to Prince Unagi, leader of the Eel
people. Their marriage is arranged as a
means to bring peace to two kingdoms. But
when Azuri falls in love with Thalo, a royal
Orcan guard, her world falls apart!

In stores NOW!

Genre Icon: Romance
Rating: Y (Youth)
Price: $4.99

sea princess
azuri
Glossary

Here are some terms you need to know in *Sea Princess Azuri...*

Merwhale - A merperson who breathes air.

Sealicorn - The ocean realm's version of the unicorn. A horned beast with the body of a large seal.

Orcan - The mermaid race that is part killer whale.

Eel - The mermaid race that is part eel.

Orca - The kingdom of the Orcans.

Bubblecloth - A breathing device used by the Orcans that fits over the nose and mouth.

Echo Clicks - The sound of the echolocation (sonar) used by dolphins and Orcans.

Jellysquid - A monster that is half jellyfish, half giant squid--and always hungry.

Breath Blast - A powerful attack only Orcans can use. It creates sound vibrations so intense they shatter almost anything.

Pod - A group of whales or merwhales.

Siren Soldier - The cavalry of the Ocean army. These soldiers have the most powerful Breath Blast attacks.

Royal Guard - The elite of the Orcan army who guard the palace and the royal family.

Gillenok - The kingdom of the Eels.

Chapter
two

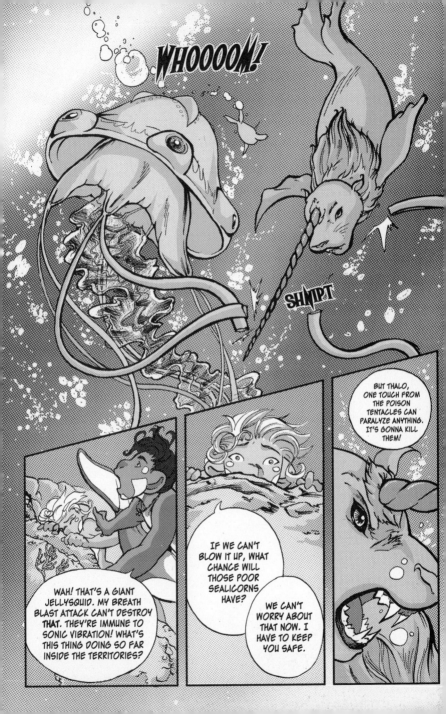

TOKYOPOP SHOP

WWW.TOKYOPOP.COM/SHOP

HOT NEWS!
Check out the TOKYOPOP SHOP! The world's best collection of manga in English is now available online in one place!

SOKORA REFUGEES T-SHIRT

LOVE HINA NOVEL

+ANIMA

WWW.TOKYOPOP.COM/SHOP

- LOOK FOR SPECIAL OFFERS
- PRE-ORDER UPCOMING RELEASES
- COMPLETE YOUR COLLECTIONS

© Rivkah and TOKYOPOP Inc.

STEADY BEAT
BY RIVKAH

"Love Jessica"... That's what Leah finds on the back of a love letter to her sister. But who is Jessica? When more letters arrive, along with flowers and other gifts, Leah goes undercover to find out her sister's secret. But what she doesn't expect is to discover a love of her own—and in a very surprising place!

Winner of the Manga Academy's Create Your Own Manga competition!

JUSTICE N MERCY
BY MIN-WOO HYUNG

Min-Woo Hyung is one of today's most talented young Korean artists, and this stunning art book shows us why. With special printing techniques and high-quality paper, TOKYOPOP presents never-before-seen artwork based on his popular *Priest* series, as well as images from past and upcoming projects *Doomslave*, *Hitman* and *Sal*.

A spectacular art book from the creator of *Priest!*

© MIN-WOO HYUNG

© 2003 Liu GOTO © SOTSU AGENCY • SUNRISE • MBS

MOBILE SUIT GUNDAM SEED NOVEL
ORIGINAL STORY BY HAJIME YATATE AND YOSHIYUKI TOMINO
WRITTEN BY LIU GOTO

A shy young student named Kira Yamato is thrown in the midst of battle when genetically enhanced Coordinators steal five new Earth Force secret weapons. Wanting only to protect his Natural friends, Kira embraces his Coordinator abilities and pilots the mobile suit Strike. The hopes and fears of a new generation clash with the greatest weapons developed by mankind: Gundam!

The novelization of the super-popular television series!

SGT FROG WANTS YOU!

SGT FROG
KERORO GUNSOU

A WACKY MANGA OF ALIEN FROGS & WORLD DOMINATION
BY MINE YOSHIZAKI